This YEAR, there is more than a THREE TIMES GREATER chance of you being **involved in a LAWSUIT** than of your being admitted into the hospital! Yet, most Americans have health and hospitalization insurance, insurance on their car, on their house, on their BOAT, but if they get sued—win or lose—it WILL *cost them money*. **The color of justice is, without a doubt, GREEN!**

The average income-earner is wary of seeking legal advice because the COST of even *visiting* an attorney is frightening. If you're in ANY kind of business, even just ALIVE, you stand a chance of being sued for any number of unforseen reasons. Often, if you lose, you could lose EVERYTHING!

Every DAY, *innocent* people are being sued for the most ridiculous reasons, and LOSING! Chances are in your favor of NOT losing if you have competent legal counsel to call upon.

How would YOU like to have the BEST legal representation money can buy—*to have your own attorney* from one of those high priced law firms—for less that a dollar per DAY?

And how would you like to be in business for yourself, and EARN money while *helping* others? This book, Part 1 and Part 2, tells both! Interested in finding out the facts?

Let's begin.

Justice is Green

Pre-Paid Legal

by

PETE BILLAC

Swan Publishing

Author: Pete Billac
Editor: Debra Merry
Cover Design: John Gilmore
Layout Design: Sharon Davis

OTHER BOOKS BY PETE BILLAC

The Annihilator
How Not to Be Lonely
How Not to Be Lonely—TONIGHT
The Last Medal of Honor
All About Cruises
New Father's Baby Guide
Lose Fat While You Sleep
Willie the Wisp
Managing Stress
The Silent Killer
The New Millionaires

Copyright @ October 2000
Swan Publishing
Library of Congress Catalog Card #00-
ISBN# 0-943629-48-9

Justice Is Green, is available through SWAN Publishing, 1059 CR 100, Burnet, TX 78611. Call at: (512) 756-6800, Fax (512) 756-0102 or e-mail: swanbooks@ghg.net

Printed in the United States of America.

FOREWORD

This is my 50th book with 45 bestsellers. I am neither smug, pompous nor arrogant over that fact; I am absolutely *thrilled.* When I pass the mirror and take a side glance I just grin at my good fortune sometimes thinking, "*You sonofagun. YOU did it!*" Then giggle all over myself.

I'm truthful and I'm candid; I tell it *like it is.* I'm giving you advanced warning so you won't feel insulted if I hit a nerve. My candor offends some, but I mean no harm; I want to help.

Do I LIKE attorneys? Some of my closest friends are attorneys. I LOVE them (when I'm in trouble and they represent ME).

Do I trust the legal system? Of course **NOT!** I trust the SMART attorney to help me THROUGH the legal system.

Do I think the legal system is fair? NO! It is definitely GREEN!

As you probably already noticed, I write with *italics*, CAPITALIZATION, **bold,** —'s, and with "quotation marks." I get letters, faxes, e-mails and telephone calls ALL THE TIME commenting on my how I break all the rules of correct writing. All I want to do with *my writing* is to COMMUNICATE!

I am chastised, commented on, even *ridiculed* for my STYLE of writing by *pure* writers, English teachers, grammarians and any number of authors, NONE of whom who have ever written a best seller.

I write so people can understand (and not **mis**-understand or **mis**-interpret) what I'm trying to say.

And THAT is why I put *emphasis* on the words that I feel are important.

Again, many professional writers say they can make their point using normal, *accepted* punctuation. Oh, yeah! Try saying what you mean in *this* sentence without making one word, each time, **bold**. Here, I'll do it for you. See how the emphasis on ONE word changes the entire context of the sentence.

I NEVER SAID HE STOLE THAT.

I never said he stole that.
I **never** said he stole that.
I never **said** he stole that.
I never said **he** stole that.
I never said he **stole** that.
I never said he stole **that!**

When I find anything that HELPS people, I write about it. This book is just such a case. I had HEARD of *Pre-Paid Legal* for at least 15 or more years. In fact, while relocating, I found "stuff" I never recall receiving or keeping. THREE DIFFERENT TIMES over the years I had received information on *Pre-Paid* Legal. I MEANT to join, but never did until about four or so months ago; until I stopped and LISTENED.

Since, I tried my best to count the dozens and dozens of times I could have used the advice of an attorney, certainly a LETTER that was written BY an attorney. AND, when I looked at checks on bills I had PAID attorneys over the years, well, it was enough to take several LONG vacations with my entire family. Had I been a member of *Pre-Paid Legal*, I'd have saved at least $100,000.

Before you get too far into this book, I'd like to put one fact to rest. I am writing this book because I *like* to write, and because I feel it will help many. I don't think any of the corporate officers in *Pre-Paid Legal* even KNOW that I'm writing this book.

Do I WORK for *Pre-Paid Legal*? **NO!** Do I get PAID by *Pre-Paid Legal*? **NO!** Have they PAID me to write this book? **NO!** Do they tell me what to say? **Of course NOT!** Do I get ANY benefit from writing this book? **I certainly HOPE so! It's my business to write and sell books.** Do I make ANYTHING if you join *Pre-Paid Legal*? **NO!**

With that behind us, let me tell you WHAT the benefits are in *Pre-Paid* Legal for YOU.

If you are in that UPPER 10% of income earners, you can *afford* to have your own attorney and you probably already have one.

If you're in the LOWER 10%, you get *free* legal *aid* from the courts. You probably will never see this book because you probably don't read and you have food, clothing and shelter to pay for, not spend ten-bucks on a book.

And, these folks, this lower 10%, can't afford ANY "paid for" legal aid and thus, the JAILS are *crowded* with those who could NOT afford their own attorney. The color of justice IS, without a doubt, GREEN! Don't EVER think it isn't!

MOST OF US—you 80% out there—NEED to read this book. Hopefully, it will SELL you on the idea of finding out MORE about *Pre-Paid Legal* to learn how truly necessary and affordable it is and how it can SAVE YOU MONEY!

Pete Billac

TABLE OF CONTENTS

PART 1
THE COST OF JUSTICE

PART 2
THE PROFITS OF JUSTICE

Why Do People Fail?
Pre-Paid Legal
Impressive Statistics
Linear versus Residual Income
Is This Network Marketing?

Dave Savula   David Breurd
Sunil Wadhwa   Les and Lorie Harrell
Jae Hoglund   Dianne Moore/David Combs
Cleve Pickens   Larry Smith
The Dorseys   John Bird
Myrna Riley   Ryan Nelson
Mark Brown   Joe Lemire

Sports Fans

Make A Grand Living/Make A Giant Difference
Make Big Money Fast
Your Test

PART 1

Chapter 1

WHO NEEDS AN ATTORNEY?

_____

All through my life—and yours if you'll think about it—there were times when we *needed* legal advice but passed on it because lawyers COST TOO MUCH. Or, we just didn't take the *time* to seek competent legal advice because we were INNOCENT and we relied upon the legal *system* of JUSTICE! Then, we went to court and pled our own cause and we LOST!

THE *COLOR* OF JUSTICE IS GREEN!

LEGAL COSTS

Most of middle-income America (about 80%-85%) is *intimidated* by lawyers. We *hear* about their exorbitant fees and we are TERRIFIED! One New York law firm hired a recent graduate with a STARTING SALARY of 110 THOUSAND DOLLARS per YEAR—STARTING salary! And WHO pays for THAT? YOU DO, of course.

And THAT recent law school graduates charge $100 an hour, MINIMUM. WAIT! The BIG guys in huge firms cost as much as $300 an hour UP! For them to *type a letter* for you, they charge $250 or **$500.** Who in the world can afford THAT? THAT scares ME!

There is a NEED for legal counsel often; we NEED one of those *doggoned*, high-priced lawyers to help us in everyday life whether we're in business for ourselves or not. From time to time, we NEED to at least *talk to* someone who knows the law. It is not wise to *guess* at it or rely on our innocence and *hope* to obtain justice through the legal system.

In the last four months alone I have had FIVE instances where an attorney helped me. Oh, I wouldn't have gone to jail, but in the past I've spent sleepless nights worrying about *things* that a mere phone call for the correct information could have settled—and did.

In today's world somebody is suing somebody else for just about anything. We're in what they call a *litigious* society. Now don't be frightened at that word, it's probably the biggest one I'll use in this book. I write in BIG print, using LITTLE words you don't need a *law degree* or a dictionary to read. I research my subjects like *Columbo,* and I go right for the jugular.

I, personally, get sued for everything! (Guess I'm *active.*) For example, some "person" sent a friend of mine a QUIZ that was almost utter nonsense and asked me to use it in one of my books. I changed it a bit, added it to some pages that I should have left *blank,* and the guy SUED me for using HIS poem.

Another time I was in "legal trouble" was when I hired a bright *bum* to do some editing and computer work for me; I paid him by CONTRACT LABOR! He did not work on a regular basis: he never showed up at any certain time; he did much of the work from his *garage/home*, and I paid him CASH (that I paid taxes on). But he fell upon even worse times and he tried to collect unemployment.

I *thought* it was legal. And, like most people, I never bothered to find out for certain because it had NO EFFECT on ME and it gave HIM more money. I had, however, just become a *member* of *Pre-Paid Legal* and their (MY) attorney gave me the correct advice and procedure and I handled it myself. I'm now 100% LEGAL.

A neighborhood kid jumped my fence, climbed a tree in my backyard, and fell out of the tree breaking his arm. You guessed it! His parents sued ME! I should have sued THEM for their kid trespassing. Again, a simple CALL from my attorney settled that and my homeowner's insurance paid for the injury. NO personal lawsuit.

My wife was backing up her BRAND NEW, three-day-old Toyota 4-runner. Some man (who turned out to be a real jerk) looking for *his* wife to come out of a store, ran into HER (not his WIFE, my wife's CAR). Of course, HE sued, claiming she backed into HIM! We had witnesses, but we still needed an attorney to represent us.

And, we just sold our house but the people who bought it wanted to SUE us for taking out a USED REFRIGERATOR worth maybe $500. It wasn't part of the sales contract. I took it for my BARN! Then, the new owners sent me a letter from *their* attorney. It was a misunderstanding developing into a headache. So MY new (*Pre-Paid Legal*) attorney hit them with HIS letter and the matter was resolved.

This kind of *stuff* happens EVERY DAY to good people who do NOT have legal representation. I HATE to see really NICE people TAKE this pushing—this abuse—from rude and unfair *jerks* who are IN business and who GET AWAY WITH IT! Well, NOT ANYMORE! NOT with members of *Pre-Paid Legal!*

YOU DON'T HAVE TO TAKE IT

There is NO REASON for YOU to ever be taken advantage of again. Or scared, or bullied, or forced into taking something you don't want because NOW, you CAN afford your OWN attorney!

Why WOULDN'T everyone and *anyone* want their own attorney to step in and handle any number of everyday problems? That's simple to answer; the COST? Well *Pre-Paid Legal* is so VERY low that you can't afford NOT to do it!

Even if you don't have a BUSINESS, if you have a good-paying job and some money saved, if you have stock, properties, an inheritance, drive your car, shop at the mall, order things, have CHILDREN, this world has become a place where you NEED an attorney and I can tell you how to get the BEST lawyers in your state for an unbelievably low cost.

It is SMART to have an attorney because you WILL sleep better. It saves you TIME to have an attorney; let THEM read and keep current with the law and you do whatever business you're good at. Having your own attorney gives you a feeling of safety.

It's even a *prestige* thing; while at a party you can mention that "*MY attorney said this or MY attorney said that.*" Not *too* often now with that statement or people will think you're *affected*; just let it drop ONE time and they'll remember it.

Yes, it's a different world out there than it was at the time *Gianinni* started the Bank of America and made loans on a handshake. Sharks are not only in the sea. They are *everywhere! YOU get sued for ANY reason and for absolutely NO reason.*

You all know of that *McDonald's* "coffee spilling" incident. The "judge shows" are as popular on TV now as are the soap operas. Look at a few of those and get a new perspective on life. Kids are suing their parents. Husbands suing wives. Brothers suing brothers. Students suing teachers. SOME people are suing their MINISTER!

YOU ARE BEING SUED

If YOU were involved in one of these lawsuits guilty OR innocent, SUING or BEING sued—WHERE do you go for legal advice without shelling out a few hundred dollars after the 10-minute FREE consultation? And that's but the INITIAL payment; there WILL be others to follow close behind.

THINK how many instances in the past year alone that YOU needed *legal advice* or *legal representation*. THINK of the times in the recent past where you NEEDED legal *information* to be able to make an informed decision that could have saved or caused you to receive more money.

But, woefully, you "passed on it" because they did not explain the legal part that would have protected you. This next chapter has but SOME of the MANY things that can happen to you in everyday life. It isn't long, it's fun (as long as it doesn't happen to you). Then—THEN—I'll tell you what *kind* of attorneys you get with *Pre-Paid Legal* and why YOU should be a part of it.

PART 1

Chapter 2

WHY DO I NEED AN ATTORNEY?

I am a law-abiding citizen. I never get in fights, argue or try to start trouble in any form or fashion. I have no need to be represented by an attorney. I live by the *Golden Rule, "Do unto others as you would* HAVE THEM *do unto you."* That's inspirational, but the two words that stand out—HAVE THEM.

You are truly a wonderful and extremely fortunate person never to have been sued, gypped, everything you bought was perfect, you had no trouble in returning items, your car repairs were made on time and your neighbors were pillars of the community. Let me guess. You're a *Trappist Monk?*

I, too, am a law-abiding citizen. But, if you will, step into MY life for a moment, the REAL world. It will also help you to understand more of my "warped" personality and make what I say (or the way I *say* it) easier to understand.

This first incident is a bit *bizarre* but true. About

a month ago I tried to close the deal on a ranch I was buying and found out that one acre was *claimed* by an INDIAN who squatted on the land 20 years ago! For TWENTY YEARS he has lived on the former owner's land. He hadn't bought the land. *He just lived there.*

He had a "house" built on it with lumber and tin he had stolen. He had a generator for lights, a refrigerator and **TV** (stolen), and food that he "confiscated" daily as it came strolling by. He had a DEAL! He didn't work, he had NO bills, he just LIVED and he was happy.

The attorney handling the transaction for the *seller* knew about it *last week* but didn't inform me until I was sitting across his desk. "*Come back Thursday. We'll have it settled by then. You'll only have to pay $17,000 more* (for ONE acre of hilly, rocky land) *in order to get the title to it!*"

Now this was MY position. I was buying the ranch for CASH. I saw the place, negotiated through the real estate listing agent, signed the contract, put up earnest money, the seller signed the contract, I had a cashier's check for the balance and THIS attorney knew there was a *glitch* LAST WEEK and didn't inform me!

I canceled several appointments, I DROVE five hours there and five hours back and he tells me he knew about this last WEEK . . . and to come back in three days (drive ANOTHER 10 hours)! No matter how much I wanted to *punch the guy out*, I had several choices:

1. Continue on with the deal and pay the extra money,
2. Forget about it and buy some other ranch,
3. Get my OWN attorney and settle it in court, "or,"
4. Try to work it out with the Indian.

I had already SCHEDULED the moving van so if I canceled at the last minute I'd lose my deposit and THEY might SUE. The guy who bought MY house had ONE DAY to get his kids enrolled in a new school and he was planning to move IN the house I sold him. He had sold HIS house, HIS furniture was scheduled to be moved in three days and HE had to find a place to live. WHO was responsible for what? SOMEBODY was going to get sued.

My options: I could settle it ALL for $17,000, pay the Indian his "squatters-rights" extortion money, and let things go as scheduled. I HATE being *held up,* and to pay such a sum for land worth maybe $400 an acre is not what I do. My *Pre-Paid Legal* attorney (I reached him in SEVEN minutes) said, the Indian could hold it up in court for MONTHS! I'd win, but look at the trouble.

After about 20 minutes of talking with MY attorney and listening to someone tell me the LEGAL options, I was able to make a decision. I WANTED that ranch, I HAD to move in a few days, I did NOT want to sue the Indian (what could I collect anyway?), and I would not pay him $17,000 for my own land.

I met with the Indian (Joe about 70 years YOUNG and quite bright) and we made a deal. I told him he could STAY on the land. I then HIRED him for

$50 a week to care for my pet animals. He agreed to ASK for things he needed to survive, and he agreed to steal from *other* ranchers.

NOW, I can show people my ranch in its entirety; my horses, my cows, my chickens, my goats, AND my INDIAN! (I wish his name was *Thunder Horse* or *Running Buffalo* but I guess "Joe" is okay). Joe and I have become friends and I invite him over for lunch or dinner at least once a week. No need to ask HIM to bring anything, chances are high that it will be from *my* ranch anyway.

Think of your OWN situation—simple, everyday happenings. A neighborhood kid gets hurt in your yard. Your *precious angel* throws a ball and hits another kid in the face breaking glasses or teeth. The store will not allow you to return the merchandise that was damaged because you don't have a receipt.

You had a ticket on a cruise ship and they *canceled* within a week from the scheduled time of embarkation, but they will RE-schedule you on *another* ship at another *time*. You chipped a tooth at a seafood restaurant. You slipped in the supermarket on some mayonnaise that was not wiped up sufficiently after the jar broke.

A delivery man backed his truck into your garage door. You SAW him but he denies doing it. Your neighbor is *usurping* a few feet of *your* property with their new fence. They have a small, positively *ugly* dog that barks all the time in a high-pitched tone and it drives you *berserk*. Another dog is running loose and bites your visiting relative. The plumber forced a fitting on a pipe and broke the entire wash basin, and wants YOU to pay for the new one.

OR, somebody falls in YOUR store. Your employee insults a customer, or *brushes* their car with YOUR truck and they want a *new car* for theirs that should be in the *Smithsonian.*

The following, silly as some may seem, HAPPEN ALL THE TIME! I could fill this entire book with examples of what happens to everyday people daily.

THINGS THAT HAPPEN IN YOUR HOME

■ An INSURANCE MAN comes in your door and slips on your newly waxed floor.

■ You SHOOT someone who was climbing in your bedroom window.

■ You are called for jury duty and would rather NOT go (for any number of reasons).

■ Your landlord inspects your apartment or condo without your permission.

■ Some jewelry is missing and you KNOW it's the cleaning lady. What are your legal options?

■ You get books or CD's sent to you AFTER you canceled your subscription, OR, you never TOOK OUT a subscription!

- You need a letter written by an attorney.

- Credit is denied and you have a good credit history.

- You DON'T have a will.

- You need a PATENT for an invention, or a COPY-RIGHT for your new bestseller.

- The carpet you ORDERED is NOT what was delivered. Yeah, *bait and switch*. Do you pay and THEN sue? Do you NOT pay? You already ripped up your OLD carpet, what are THEY responsible for?

- You are planning to SELL your home and buy another one. (NO Indian is involved.)

- You have "some" money and your *intended* does not. What about a prenuptial agreement?

- You are getting a divorce. On Adultery? YOU are the culprit! THEY are.

- Your spouse hits you.

- A MINOR is caught breaking into your home.

- Your deceased spouse left NO WILL!

- Your LIVING spouse claims a right to your earnings.

■   Your NEW HOME has "problems." Doors don't close. The garage opener doesn't work. The walls have "bumps." The air conditioner doesn't cool sufficiently. MANY things do not work.

■   A repair person charges more than the estimate and refuses to leave AFTER he installed whatever-it-is you ordered.

■   You are ARRESTED at your home for no apparent reason.

■   Your landlord raises your rent violating a *verbal* agreement.

■   A piece of furniture was damaged in shipment and the mover won't pay for the damage.

■   You plan to ADOPT!

■   You can't get your *cleaning deposit* back from the condo you leased for two years.

■   The movers LOST something of yours during the move.

■   FAMILY members *challenge* your parents' will.

■   A STRANGER calls and demands money or they will release damaging information about you.

NEIGHBORS AND YOUR YARD

- Your neighbor curses your kids.

- A pool repair person doesn't fix your pool and has been out *three times!* You do not want them there again and you do not want to pay the bill for NOT making the repairs.

- A *neighbor's child* bites YOUR child. Your DOG bites a *neighbor's* child. The *neighbor's child* bites your DOG!

- Your neighbor's tree has limbs that hang over your fence and *nearing* the roof on your garage or house.

- A neighbor throws WILD, LOUD parties—often!

- A neighbor is a PIG and refuses to clean or mow around their house, lowering property values in your neighborhood.

- A neighbor steps on a rake in your yard and gets banged in the head and needs stitches.

- Your dog is poisoned!

- Your neighbor reports you for CHILD ABUSE.

- Your neighbor's dog attacks and injures/kills your dog.

■ YOUR dog bites a passerby, or frightens an elderly person and they fall, hurting themselves.

■ Your dog tramples a neighbor's garden.

■ Your neighbor is building a *tool shed* on YOUR property line.

■ Your neighbor is building a TEN-FOOT HIGH fence and it blocks your view.

THINGS THAT HAPPEN WHILE YOU ARE
Shopping/Driving/Dining

■ The store refuses to take back the damaged (or unwanted) merchandise.

■ A store refuses to sell you an article for the amount LISTED on the tag.

■ You almost choke on a fish (or chicken) bone at a restaurant.

■ You're the victim of a *hit-and-run*; you get their license number.

■ Your hair is RUINED in a beauty shop because of harsh chemicals.

■ Your coat (purse, sweater) is stolen while you are at a restaurant.

■   You want to buy (or sell) a car.

■   You are asked to identify a robber and appear at the trial.

■   You are involved in a FIGHT where you hit someone and elect NOT to go before Judge Judy.

■   An ARGUMENT turns into a slander suit.

■   Your car is vandalized and the parking lot manager has a NOT RESPONSIBLE sign posted.

■   You are refused service at a restaurant.

■   Your car door is knocked off by a speeding car when you are parking on a public street.

■   You lose an expensive piece of jewelry in a hotel, and the manager refuses any liability.

■   You TRIP on an elevator that did not stop level with the floor.

■   YOU get a ticket for SPEEDING.

■   The cleaners lost/ruined an expensive suit.

KIDS

■   Your *teenager* gets a speeding ticket.

- They find narcotics in the car, but his/her *passenger* is carrying it.

- There is an accident. It's his/her fault. Somebody is hurt. Somebody is *killed!*

- You get hit with a foul ball at a baseball game, or by a flying bottle thrown by a spectator.

- Your daughter is dating a *jerk* and you'd like to strangle him; what ARE your legal rights?

- Your son/daughter sues YOU!

- Your kid is *accused* of shoplifting. They were *caught* shoplifting.

- Your "precious angel" put holes with his B.B. gun in your neighbor's windows.

- Your child's ball goes over the neighbor's fence and the neighbor will NOT return it.

- Your child (not MY kid) CURSES your neighbor.

- You TOLD your neighbor you didn't want their kids playing in your yard but they did, the swing broke, and there's a lawsuit.

AT THE WORKPLACE

- You THINK you are being sexually harassed.

- You are not hired because of your color.

- You are FINED for being late for work.

- You have questions about starting a new business.

- Your boss *insults* you in front of the entire office.

- Any other reasons YOU can think of (I'm getting tired of this).

AT PLAY

- YOU hit another golfer with your golf ball while at the golf course. You hit a spectator. You break a picture window on a *house* adjacent to the course. Your bad *slice* breaks a car windshield in the parking lot. The golf cart you are renting overturns on a hill and you get hurt. Your passenger gets hurt. You are not a member. You ARE a member.

- At a high-school reunion picnic, your nose is broken in a "friendly" game of *semi*-touch football.

- You're at a baseball game and get *beaned* with a long foul ball or somebody throws a can of beer at the umpire but it hits you and breaks a tooth.

■   You cheered when a bad pitch hit a player and his dad was sitting next to you. He blackened your eye.

■   You stumble on uneven cement while walking in the park and sprain your ankle.

■   A monkey at the zoo spits in your eye.

■   You backed up while standing in the popcorn line and spilled a soda on a lady's new blouse.

■   You were fishing from a pier with your kid who hooked another person fishing in the NOSE with his treble hook as he jerked it out of the water.

■   You turned the handle the wrong way and instead of slowing you ran your friend's new boat into the bulkhead.

■   While water skiing, you ran over someone who was floating on an inner tube.

■   While deer hunting, you shot a rancher's GOAT instead of a Buck.

This list goes on and ON and **ON!** THINK of these everyday happenings and what are YOUR chances of them happening to you? ALL have happened to *somebody!* I got it from the law library.

What was one way yesterday is a different way today—and chances are it could change tomorrow.

That's why I advised earlier on, to LET YOUR ATTOR-NEY keep up with these changes and laws. Don't "wonder" what is right and wrong, don't LOSE SLEEP over it and stress yourself out, and for goodness sakes, don't let it cost you ANY of your hard-earned money. This *Pre-Paid Legal* stuff is EASY to obtain and it is **IN**-EXPENSIVE.

If you need a heart operation, don't ask a FRIEND; go to a *heart surgeon!* If you want to lose weight, why ask a *fat* person how to do it? If you want to get rich, how can you possibly listen to some *homeless person* tell you how to go about it? If you want LEGAL advice—which you WILL need OF-TEN—get YOUR OWN ATTORNEY!

SERIOUS STUFF

I am not cynical. I am factual, pragmatic, a realist. If YOU disagree that justice is ANY color other than *green*, you're an idiot! Or, too naive to even *have* an opinion. In my research I visited jails, and sat in courtrooms, and listened to people, *kids*—mostly minorities get advice from the "legal counselors" whom the courts appoint for those who cannot afford to pay, that lower 10% of our income structure.

WHERE, do these people COME from? These Public *offenders*, I mean Public DEFENDERS? Surely they didn't become this non caring overnight? Were they LAST in their class at law school? Did they have to take the bar exam a dozen times and then just skim by? What did they DO to get stuck in this position?

Years ago I've seen them try to rush a 19-year-old black kid into a decision that would have sent him to jail for TWO years for having a marijuana joint in his pocket, by scaring him with a longer prison term because the jerk "prison attorney" would have been late for a luncheon date.

Chances are high that, that 19-year-old "kid" would have come out of that prison in two years a learned and hardened criminal.

I couldn't allow that. I called my attorney and for $500 and legal representation (that took maybe 20 minutes), the boy was given a *suspended sentence* with 150 hours of community service. I never saw the boy again. Justice IS green! Perhaps YOU will never be in this position, but it is for that 10% at the bottom of the financial *totem* pole.

Jails are filled mostly with people who wouldn't be there IF they had MONEY, or some type of legal representation. This isn't to say they are innocent; many are certainly guilty of *some* crime, but the *lengths* of these sentences are cruel and unwarranted. IF many of these people had money (that GREEN stuff) they would at least have had a CHANCE to prove their innocence or get a lesser punishment that matched the severity of their crime.

No need to tell you more. You've heard it, you've read about it, and some of you have *witnessed* it in any number of instances. But what about YOU? How can YOU be hurt if you're a law-abiding citizen and you are arrested, or "detained," or accused of, or being SUED for something of which you are totally innocent?

And yes, ONLY the top 10 percent of Americans—the rich or the large corporations—can *afford* the services of the BEST lawyers. NOW, with *Pre-Paid Legal* rearing it's wondrous head from out of nowhere, you can HAVE the best for less than **one dollar a day!** Unbelievable, isn't it?

These giant corporations and the ones who head them have lawyers on retainers, GOOD lawyers; in fact, the very BEST lawyers money can buy and these SAME attorneys can be YOURS for less than a FRACTION of the normal cost.

You see, with *Pre-Paid Legal* you have sort of *consortium.* (I used to pronounce it con-sort-ti-um but now, I understand that it's pronounced consor-shum) Everyone POOLS their money and the *Pre-Paid Legal* folks hire TOP law firms with TOP lawyers who SPECIALIZE in whatever your problem might be. AND, they are available to you. They are waiting for your call, *expecting* it, and they treat you with the same respect as they do the CEO of a giant corporation. Here's how THAT works.

Chapter 3

YOUR $25 A MONTH ATTORNEY

If you are in the majority, a middle-class American, how likely is it that you'll end up in court? Statistics tell us that more than 33 million Americans go to the hospital each year, but **ONE HUNDRED MILLION** Americans end up in court!

There are 273,972 court filings per DAY! That works out to be 11,415 per HOUR, 190 each MINUTE, so YOUR chances are high that you'll be in this spot. According to the *American Bar Association*, more than HALF the households in America are facing a legal situation this very SECOND. *The National Resources Center for Consumers of Legal Services* states that *"even LAW ABIDING Americans will encounter a potential legal situation four to six times per year."*

MOST who cannot afford an attorney (or don't think they can) will either ignore the problem or try to handle it themselves. When it comes to the need for legal services, it is not a question of IF but WHEN.

Your ODDS of it happening to YOU are far too great to chance NOT having your own attorney.

You have NO IDEA how powerful a telephone call or letter from an attorney is! It *stopped* FIVE "potential problems" in my life in the past three months. I already HAD my own attorney. However, he's my friend and if he doesn't charge me I feel bad and if he charges too much, I feel WORSE!

Now, that I'M a member of *Pre-Paid Legal*, I truly feel "safe"and I USE them. I like to SAVE money, I like a DEAL and the DEAL OF THE CENTURY is my *Pre-Paid Legal*.

ARE THE ATTORNEYS GOOD?

Yes! YES! And **YES!** The best in the business. Let me tell you why. I had to "borrow" this from a book "THE PRE-PAID LEGAL STORY" about Harland C. Stonecipher, founder of *Pre-Paid Legal*. The book tells how he began in this business and how the business has progressed. Fine book. Get it. It's a success story told in such a way that you will enjoy reading it.

Mr. Stoneciphers' story about the attorneys is said in a way that I can't top. So, I'm using it. I'm quoting him, word for word. Hope I'm not sued. If so, it's my *Pre-Paid Legal* attorney against his.

"When I first started going to Wall Street to try to interest investors in *Pre-Paid Legal* going on the stock exchange, one analyst asked me . . . "

"*Tell me, Mr. Stonecipher, what do these $15-a-month lawyers **look** like?*"

"Mike Turpen, a former state attorney general of Oklahoma said," "*Harland, next time he asks you that, tell him A MILLION BUCKS! Because that's what you paid me last year.*"

That was six years ago. This year he is paying Mike's law firm **THREE** million!

In Texas, for example, *Pre-Paid Legal* is paying one firm $750,000—per MONTH. "Soon," Mr. Stonecipher said, "it will be a MILLION a month! There is not a law firm in this country whose attention you can't get for a million dollars a month. THAT'S what *Pre-Paid Legal's* $15-a-month lawyers look like!"

As a member of *Pre-Paid Legal*, will they listen to you? BET ON IT!

WHAT DO YOU GET WITH PRE-PAID LEGAL?

There is a GROUP PLAN you can get for as little as $14.95 per month (for five or more in a company or business or club). This price is the SAME as it was back in 1985. You get representation from top-quality law firms in America. And it's not just access—it's UNLIMITED access—and not only for YOU, but for your ENTIRE FAMILY! Call as many times as you want during normal business hours.

Since I'm "active" and opinionated and *stick my nose where it doesn't belong*, I took the BIG *kahuna* and I pay $25 a month. If you're not in a group, this is what I recommend for you, too.

1. UNLIMITED PHONE CONSULTATIONS:

You get an attorney from a *leading* law firm who SPECIALIZES in what your problem is. Dial a toll-free number, gave the Customer Service Representative your personal ID #, tell them the problem area, and an attorney will call you back within the next 24 hours; *most of the time* in mere HOURS!

I made five calls about my problems; they called me back in two hours, three hours, seven hours, and on the other two, in 15 MINUTES! IF it's an EMER-GENCY, tell the *Customer Service Representative* who will act (react) accordingly. AND, if you make a call and the telephone rings more than THREE TIMES and someone doesn't answer it with a LIVE voice, TELL THE COMPANY ABOUT IT!

MOST of the problems MOST people have can be "handled" without being "settled" in court. And a phone call to find out WHAT your options are is invaluable. You have YOUR attorney to ask these questions and they are only a phone call away. You have UNLIMITED phone calls.

Since you have an UNLIMITED number of subjects and times to CALL, your "Provider Attorney" (that's their general title) will determine—on the spot—whether you need ADVICE ONLY from him, or you need HIM to make a call on your behalf.

When someone gets a call from *your* ATTOR-NEY, they listen, they reconsider, they settle or drop their lawsuit or intended lawsuit. It happens time and time again. This service is AWESOME!

2. LETTERS:

OR, your attorney will determine if you need him to WRITE A LETTER in your behalf. You are entitled to but TWO of these letters or phone calls (from your attorney) per membership year. Any additional ones you pay for MINUS 25%.

Note: *That's not such a big deal, you say? Get real! There HAS to be a limit. Some "cuckoo birds" would ask for a telephone call or a letter written for them DAILY! Whereas, you have unlimited phone calls TO the attorney and 95% of the general problems can be handled with the correct, expert, legal advice you get over the telephone. UNLIM- ITED CALLS!*

3. CONTRACT AND DOCUMENT REVIEW:

You may have your *Provider Attorney* REVIEW any personal legal document (10 pages or less), and one BUSINESS DOCUMENT (10 pages or less), per mem- bership year.

Note: *I like to answer any questions I THINK you might be thinking without delay. Hopefully, you are NOT going to be sued, buy or sell a house, or "get in trouble" on a daily basis. There MUST be some restrictions or the entire system would not work!*

4. WILL PREPARATION:

EVERYONE should have a Last Will and Testament; this protects YOUR FAMILY! I just had a will prepared last year and it cost me $500 from a friend/attorney. YOURS goes along with your $14.95 (or $25 membership) with UPDATES done on it yearly!

For any OTHER member of your family covered under your membership, THEIR Last Will and Testament will be prepared for TWENTY DOLLARS!

5. MOTOR VEHICLE RELATED BENEFITS:

If you are driving a car (bus, truck) with the express consent and permission of the owner and you have a wreck, or get a ticket for a *moving* violation, you get:

✔ A defense from your attorney.

✔ Defense of any criminal charges for Manslaughter, Negligent or Vehicular Homicide.

✔ You also get 2½ hours of "attorney's time" when:

- ► **Your driver's license is canceled or refused.**
- ► **You need to reinstate or keep your license because of job-related matters.**
- ► **You need to reinstate your driver's license for medical reasons.**

ALSO, your attorney will sue to collect all personal injury and property damage claims of $2,000 or less as a result of your riding in, driving, or being *struck by a motor vehicle or boat* up to 2½ hours of attorney time per claim.

6. TRIAL DEFENSE BENEFIT:

If you or your spouse is a defendant in a CIVIL action or in a *covered* (the contract spells out what IS and what is NOT covered) criminal action filed in a state or federal court for a JOB RELATED incident like a wage, salary, or bonus dispute, your attorney will come to your aid.

WHO ARE THESE ATTORNEYS?

Yeah, how do you find these attorneys that you say are in some of the most prestigious law firms in the nation?

They are recommended by other attorneys; through *Pre-Paid Legal's* investigation through the bar association, client reference, and personal *visits* to law firms for personal evaluation. ALL of these firms are rated by *Martindale-Hubbard,* who has rated the legal community for over a century. They interview lawyers and judges and get confidential opinions on the abilities and ethics of these law firms and their lawyers.

Each member of the provider firm has an 8-year on average experience as an attorney. Not that "new" lawyers aren't good, it's just the same as if you are going to have a *heart-transplant* and a young doctor comes in and smiles. *"Hi, this is my FIRST OPERA-TION. You have nothing to worry about."*

Pre-Paid Legal gets the best attorneys there are because of MONEY! Not only is the color of JUSTICE green, but the color of justice that REPRESENTS YOU THE BEST, is also green. That's the way life is; if you want the BEST of anything, you PAY for it.

How can your little "less than a dollar a day"get you the BEST? Because the *pool* of more than **ONE MILLION** *Pre-Paid Legal* policyholders is all thrown into one pot. This *BUYS* CLOUT in the legal community. Firms are paid on a *per capita* basis. In MANY cases, *Pre-Paid Legal* is their BIGGEST CLIENT!

When you call, remember you are that law firm's MAJOR client and you get the same treatment (well, *almost the same*) as the CEO of a giant corporation.

Pre-Paid Legal has PAID over 150 MILLION dollars to more than 100,000 attorneys across the United States. *Pre-Paid Legal* is the MAJOR client in MOST of these firms. So when YOU call, you truly DO get preferential treatment.

Whew! I am nearly exhausted with facts and figures. If you need to know more or if you want to JOIN, go to the very LAST page in the back of this book where there is a number to call to get this infor-mation.

These people will not try to SELL you anything; the facts in this book should do that. They will only TELL you HOW to do it so YOU can sleep well at night, so YOU will not lose what you have, and so you can get the TREATMENT—under the law—that you deserve.

In Washington, D.C., on the SUPREME COURT BUILDING, there are the words written in GRANITE (or marble) on the front of that magnificent structure:

EQUAL JUSTICE UNDER THE LAW

THOSE words, of course, are a *crock!* WHO is responsible for writing that? For SAYING that? You visit any court in the land and sit through any number of trials and watch the treatment the "poor folks" receive who use a Public Offender (or those with an in-experienced lawyer, or NO lawyer) then you tell ME what those words mean.

They should have the REAL *Golden Rule* written there:

"The one that's GOT the gold, RULES!"

Note: *EVERYTHING is subject to change. When you need the EXACT information, the person who is an associate with Pre-Paid Legal will have it all for you. THEY will have the current information. As of this date, the information is 100% correct.*

Now, let's go to Part 2 and find out how you can MAKE money working in *Pre-Paid Legal.*

PART 2

Foreword

PRE-PAID LEGAL
A HOME-BASED BUSINESS

Chances are high that you'll NEVER get rich working for somebody else; you MUST be in business for yourself. BUT, how can you POSSIBLY do it if you have NO money, NO formal education, NO prior experience and you've worked your entire life in a JOB? You can't *quit* your job, or go back to school to furnish your education; you've got a family to feed. What CAN you do?

Here, in this L-O-N-G foreword, is a story that I've carried with me for life. I don't know if it's YOUR story (I certainly hope not) but if it is—MEN you just read about Jim's side. And if you're a woman in this situation, read it from Barbara's point of view.

When I graduated from high school, two friends of mine (Jim and Barbara) decided to marry. Barbara went to work for the Louisiana Power and Light Company in New Orleans as a receptionist, and Jim worked for the same company as a telephone lineman.

As most kids do when they get their first job, they buy a new car—usually a red sports model— and they rented a small apartment. They furnished their apartment with whatever they could get on sale, complimented with a few Bean Bag chairs and a bookcase made of concrete blocks and 1 x 10 boards. Both were bright and they had their entire lives ahead of them.

Jim promised Barbara that her working would be only *temporary*. They both wanted a family and in two years when Barbara got pregnant, their first son was born. Barbara worked until the last WEEK of her pregnancy and then stayed at home with the new baby.

They never had much money saved, insurance covered the cost of *having* the baby, but now their income was cut by about 40% with Barbara not working. Both of their parents helped financially, somewhat. Babies cost MONEY; even back then. So Jim had no choice but to take a part-time job where he worked most weekends just to pay the bills.

Within a year and a few months Barbara was

expecting a second child. By the time *that* child was born, Jim had gotten a raise but STILL, the money wasn't sufficient and Jim was rarely home; he was now working THREE jobs. He promised Barbara that things would change, and they did. They got WORSE!

Three months after their third child was born, Barbara had no choice but to go back to work and Jim's mother watched the kids; 14 years later Barbara is STILL working, cleaning her own modest home, paying the mortgage, riding "herd" over their three kids and NOBODY is happy. Jim feels like a failure even though he has been a steady worker, loving husband, good father, but his initial promise to Barbara never came true.

Barbara WANTED to be at home with her kids because no grandmother, sister, neighbor, baby sitter, *nanny* or mother-in-law can't do the same for your children as their mother. *Barbara's* life was the pits! And, *Jim's* life was no better.

Jim was now putting in about 80 hours a week at his *jobs*, and when he did come home he was too tired to pay much attention to the kids *or* to Barbara. Barbara was tired, too, and BOTH of their lives were well—OVER!

Does THIS sound familiar to any of you? It's happening to TENS OF THOUSANDS of families per day. There MUST be a way out of this rut? Jim got a raise but he was still working for someone else; he had a J.O.B! Actually, he had THREE jobs.

And Jim's promise to Barbara "back then" never came true. "I'm due for another raise and soon," he told her, "you'll be able to quit your job and spend your time with the kids. I love you, honey, and I'll take care of you and our family."

Jim MEANT every word but, he was never REALLY able to *take care of her"* and Barbara continued working. In time, he and Barbara either grew farther apart or never got to really know each other. They are now divorced!

I saw Barbara about a year after their divorce when I flew in to visit my brother. I was shocked! This sweet, loving, BEAUTIFUL girl had changed; she had HARDENED! Her face showed wrinkles and worry lines, her eyes seemed cold, and she looked 20 years older than she should have. Worry and poverty have a way of doing that to people.

I called Jim; he didn't look that good either. He faked a smile and we shook hands but he, too, was a different person. Jim, sweet, caring, good person that he is, was heartbroken. He REALLY tried to make things work, he did what so many did and he ended up without a family and totally unhappy.

He visits his kids when he can, he's living in an apartment, he pays his child support and sees his kids every other weekend, and, he is STILL working for the light company. Jim was hurt on the job and has an office position with LESS pay and . . . well . . . that's it. They are both OLD at 37!

This happened to very sweet, loving, caring vibrant young people who have grown OLD before their time. Barbara, as much as Jim tried, lost respect for him and when respect goes, love flies out of the window with it.

There are three kinds of people in this world; those who WATCH things happen; those who MAKE things happen, and those who don't know WHAT'S happening. Jim was the kind who WATCHED. He had several opportunities to go into part-time businesses with friends but he would not take the chance!

I do NOT want this to happen to you. And if it is, I'm hoping my book and some of these stories motivates you into action—to TAKE A CHANCE! This segment of the book will give you some options. It could, *easily,* change your financial life forever.

If you have money problems (who doesn't?), and you're STUCK in a low-paying, no-future JOB, no formal education or experience, and you truly WANT to do something to change, there ARE options; let's find a way that you can DO for your family and they will be proud of you, and you will be proud of yourself. Remember the phrase: "**If it is to BE, it is up to ME!**" Now, Let's get to it.

Chapter 1

YOU AND YOUR FUTURE

Most people are lazy and want it "handed" to them, regardless what "it" is. They want to know how YOU are going to help THEM, how YOU are going to make THEM feel better, how YOU can help THEM live longer, healthier, happier, richer, etc. THAT is human nature and most of us are in that category.

With THIS book, I've already told you how to make your life easier and more stress free, and how to SAVE what you have, and to protect what you *plan* to have, and to do *all of this* inexpensively. NOW, let's get down to how I can guide you (through my research and experience) to become financially "fixed," and maybe become RICH.

Have I done it myself? Oh yes! And I'm going to tell you HOW, and even HELP you—IF you want to learn, IF you want to work hard and smart, and IF this is the right path for you to take. It isn't easy to become rich. It takes determination, working hard, working smart, the right *vehicle,* something that appeals to the MASSES, timing, and a little luck thrown in.

Did I mention earlier that 16 years ago I took *bankruptcy?* Yep! I went *down the tube*—but not alone. With me were the likes of former Texas governor John Connolly, famous heart surgeon Dr. Denton Cooley and a passel (bunch) of other notables. It happened to over 15,000 people in Houston alone in 1984 and 85.

I had a lot of money, but I invested in real estate and oil. *I was greedy and stupid.* When the people who owed *me* money couldn't pay, I couldn't pay the ones I owed. Yes, the ones who owed me wrote their own books; Chapter 11, Chapter 7 and Chapter 13 and I had to get out and *work* because I not only LOST everything, I OWED almost a million dollars!

I had two strong motivating factors; *hunger and loss of dignity.* It's terrible to be poor, but it is totally DEVASTATING to be rich and then BECOME poor. I could no longer "run with the pack" and consequently, I had to leave the pack—temporarily.

However, I am NOT the kind to *watch* things happen. Once I find out WHAT'S happening, I go after it. What could I do that was legal and make a lot of money? I was a writer, so why not write? If I hit a good book, I make a lot.

But then, authors are not all rich. In fact, in an article about 15 years ago in a Houston newspaper they listed "freelance writer" at 499th and MIGRANT FARM WORKER 500th for the lowest paying jobs in America. Writing a book is one thing, writing a book that SELLS is another. A MONKEY can WRITE a book; it takes a TEAM or hard-working SMART monkeys to SELL the book!

So I wrote a book titled, HOW NOT TO BE LONELY; How to FIND a mate; WHAT to look for; WHERE to look, and HOW to keep them. I worked it. I gave 677 speeches in one year to anyone or group who would listen. I got FREE newspaper interviews, FREE radio, I made it to a few TV stations and then to shows like DONAHUE, SALLY JESSY RAPHAEL, and GOOD MORNING AMERICA, among others. I didn't see my home in the DAYLIGHT for almost three years. The book grossed 51 MILLION dollars!

I was the *Rocky Balboa* of the book world. I lived it, I wrote it, I published it and I SOLD it. NOBODY (publisher or agent) would sign me because I was not a psychiatrist, psychologist, or counselor. I had "*no relevant credentials*" they said. I had NO choice; I had to publish it myself.

I put my pride in my pocket and went to friends to borrow the money to print a few thousand books. I sold those and printed 2,000 more. Then I printed 5,000, then 10,000, then 50,000. One print run was 500,000 and my book sold worldwide. WOMEN bought it 1,000 to 1 because "*Men KNOW the answers.*" WE don't need that kind of advice.

So, I printed the SAME book but with a different cover and added TONIGHT to the title; HOW NOT TO BE LONELY—TONIGHT. Men bought it 400 to 1. Human nature; women are the nesters, men are the hunters. We want to know RIGHT NOW how to "get things going." Stupid, huh? That's how we are.

"*No relevant credentials.*" That phrase will stick with me forever. Well, I *"No relevant credentialed THEM!"* Bragging? A little bit. Mostly though, I am THRILLED over it all and this affords me the time to CHOOSE what I write about and I want others to experience the financial freedom that I now have. I want to help you. Just remember, *"If it is to be, it is up to me!"*

WHY DO PEOPLE FAIL?

Most just WATCH things happen. And for those who make it and become greedy, they fail also. For MOST people who fail at ANY business, it's for three general reasons; GREEDY, LAZY or STUPID! I was never lazy, but I *was* greedy and I was stupid. And by not being LAZY, I RUSHED to make greedy and stupid decisions. Hey! I'm a human being and only you and God are perfect!

MOST people fail (financially) in LIFE! If YOU failed (or ARE failing) it's because:

- **You have NO BELIEF in your own ability.**
- **You are too LAZY to learn.**
- **You are AFRAID to take a chance.**
- **You don't know HOW to go about it.**
- **The right "vehicle" hasn't come by.**
- **You WAIT and never ACT when it does.**
- **You make EXCUSES and you don't TRY.**

I'm not trying to insult you. Put *yourself* in any of these categories. It's like an alcoholic, or a dope addict, or a liar, or an unsuccessful person who complains and moans and groans and blames *others* for their problems/failures. The FIRST thing to do is to RECOGNIZE that problem and then DEAL WITH IT!

It's NOT EASY to get rich; it takes hard, SMART work; a little luck never hurts. Most successful people, however, make their *own* luck. A fellow Houstonian, *A. J. Foyt* (famous race car driver) said,**"Luck is when opportunity meets preparation."**

If you are *not* financially successful; IF you have a JOB where you are not appreciated, where you are underpaid, overworked, but you HAVE to keep it to survive, to *keep beans on the table*, to keep up payments on the car, house, boat, etc. What ARE your options? What ARE your chances of getting out of your present *financial quagmire* and making money, gaining prestige, making life easier for yourself and your family?

REASONS FOR FAILURE

Let's take them one by one and FIND an answer TOGETHER.

● **No belief in your own ability.**

"If you think you CAN, or think you CAN'T you're right!"
It's that simple. If you do not have belief in your own ability, you are STUCK in a rut. **"The only difference between a**

rut and a GRAVE, is that with a rut you have two ways out!"

- ### ARE you just plain LAZY with NO ambition?

FIND a way—an opportunity—and perhaps, just PER-HAPS, you'll get off your lazy butt and DO something. MOST lazy people have no self-esteem, perhaps because they tried and tried again and failed. Perhaps they are SATISFIED, and if they are, and if their family is satisfied, STAY THE WAY YOU are and ENJOY being lazy! Not everyone can (or wants to be) a rocket scientist or a boss. Just know this:

"It makes no difference how many times you were knocked DOWN, it's how many times you get back UP!"

- ### You are AFRAID to take a chance to get something better.

I understand this. Perhaps you have a family to feed with bills to pay and you can't AFFORD to quit your regular job and take a CHANCE on something else. You have no education, no savings, no money to start your own busi-ness. You can't afford to go back to school. What ARE your options? Simple.

You **TRY it, PART-TIME!** You watch less TV, put your fishing pole or golf clubs in the closet for a year or so. It isn't that long a time to TAKE A CHANCE of getting out of your financial RUT forever! This way you can still feed your family and you are TRYING to begin working for yourself.

"No guts, NO glory." Take a chance. *"If you never*

TAKE a chance, you never HAVE a chance."

If you truly WANT to be financially independent, if you WANT to go into business for yourself, it is your ONLY chance to make your life a more fulfilling one financially. You can NEVER do it working for somebody else; you MUST be in business for yourself.

● **YOU don't know HOW to go about it.**

Remember the three general classifications of people in the entire world?

✓ **Ones who WATCH things happen**
✓ **Ones who MAKE things happen**
✓ **Ones who don't know WHAT'S happening!**

Well, this book gives you one FASCINATING option—*PRE-PAID LEGAL!* Work, AT home, FOR yourself and use THEIR methods. It's worked for over 28 years for hundreds of thousands of others, why not you? And, MAKE money while SAVING money!

What I'm going to do for you now is tell you WHAT'S happening. Now, you'll either continue to WATCH things happen, or you'll MAKE things happen! It reminds me about WISHING versus WANTING.

"When you WISH for something, you do nothing and only HOPE it comes along. But when you WANT something, you go after it an get it!"

● **The right "vehicle" has never come by.**

It HAS now! I plan to share testimonials with you from others who were *"stuck"* in a J-O-B, and THEY got out. SO

CAN YOU! But, not EVERYONE can make it in *Pre-Paid Legal*; it takes a SPECIAL person with SPECIAL qualifications.

- **You WAIT and never act**.

So? You're a member of the human race. Don't *beat yourself up* for being the way you are. Just CHANGE and make life easier for yourself. In fact, you ARE ready to act or you wouldn't be reading this part of this book.

You're looking, and that's the first step. You'll find something. You KNOW there are opportunities out there; this is AMERICA! How CAN you make a LOT of money? We've already established that you can't get rich working for SOMEBODY else; you MUST be in business for yourself.

PRE-PAID LEGAL

Being in your own business is the only CHANCE you have to provide for yourself and your family. It can provide your kids an education, and enables you to live "the good life" if you're successful, but some of you *cannot* work for yourself, and have NO CHOICE than to work for someone else in a regular JOB!

Do you know what the QUALIFICATIONS are for being successful in *Pre-Paid Legal*? FIRST, you must **WANT to be successful; you must have DESIRE!** Of course, that's the first rule for being successful in anything.

SECOND, **you must TRY and be willing to LEARN!** It isn't difficult and if you want it badly enough, you'll make it.

THIRD, **be (or learn to be) ORGANIZED!** This is not a JOB; this is a PROFESSION. You must LOOK like a professional, you must ACT like a professional, and you must TALK like a professional. When you do, people will respect you and LISTEN to you.

IS *Pre-Paid Legal* for you? THAT, my friend, depends solely on you! Only YOU can answer that! What I'm, telling you is that you MUST work in your own home-based business if you want success and prestige and if you want MORE for your family.

MOST new businesses don't make it the first year. That means that most PEOPLE who run their own businesses lose, make very little, or break even. With *Pre-Paid Legal*, it's been around for TWENTY-EIGHT years. Have THEY made it? Have people who are IN the business making it? Let's look at the company for a page or two.

IMPRESSIVE STATISTICS

Pre-Paid Legal is not only working, it is working PHENOMENALLY well! They are written up in some of the top magazines in the world; *Forbes, Money*, and *Fortune* are but a few. *Fortune magazine* rated *Pre-Paid Legal* as one of the fastest growing companies in America for two years in a row.

Forbes Magazine says that *Pre-Paid Legal* has been one of the 200 BEST small companies in America for the past three years. And *Money Magazine* ranked the top 50 stocks of the 90's and *Pre-Paid*

Legal ranked #13, ahead of companies like *Microsoft* (rated #17). This is no fly-by-night company.

They were the *NUMBER ONE* performing company on the *American Stock Exchange.* The CHAIRMAN of the *American Stock Exchange*, Richard F. Syron, said, *"Pre-Paid Legal is a very successful company with a great idea, but I also believe it is still at the fairly **early stages** of what I think is going to be continued strong growth."*

Early STAGES? They are in their INFANCY! The company has LESS THAN two TENTHS of ONE PERCENT of market penetration. People either aren't AWARE of *Pre-Paid Legal* or they haven't stopped to find out about it.

Now, they are on the NEW YORK STOCK EXCHANGE where they are listed as 33rd in a list of 100 of the fastest growing companies in America. They are number FOUR in the EPS (Earnings Per Share) ratings. Let's take a look at some OTHER businesses you could get into and weigh out your chances of each.

You COULD start a McDonald's franchise; they are certainly America's *success story*. That would cost you a **MILLION AND A HALF DOLLARS** to TRY, and THEN you go to work. Wonder how many Big Mac's you'd have to sell to make that million and a half BACK, you know, before YOU started *making* money?

Or, perhaps a smaller business franchise like *STARBUCKS* coffee. That would only cost you **SIX HUNDRED THOUSAND DOLLARS** (and then you would have to go to work). Now how many of the big

Latte's sold would it take to get that original 600 thousand G's back? Yes, it TAKES money to MAKE money; well, MOST OF THE TIME!

OR, you could start your own business in *Pre-Paid Legal.* To TRY costs you $249. Is it worth the risk? You work from your home. One of the people I interviewed (Sunil Wadwah) made *his* money back along with a profit of about fifty bucks in a single WEEK! His *first year* he brought in $85,000. The year after that, and the year after that, and the one after THAT, even MORE!

My "mission" is to help as many as I can earn really BIG money. Why? Because I enjoy doing it; I LIKE for people to say *"thank you"* and I feel good about myself. Do I make money in the process? Bet your boots I do. I'm nice and I'm helpful, but I'm not dumb! I make money by selling books and showing OTHERS how to be successful.

LINEAR VERSUS RESIDUAL INCOME

Know what? YOU can do it too! You know you'll NEVER do it working a JOB; that's *LINEAR* income. Which means: the more HOURS you put in, or the more you sell, or the FASTER you repair something (for someone else) the more money you make. When YOU stop, the money stops!

Whereas *RESIDUAL* income is what you must have in order to get rich. It's that simple. DUPLICATE yourself. Teach OTHERS to do as you are doing and others to do that and it works UP. Is it a Pyramid? I think so. Is it illegal? I think **NOT!** This business involves LAWYERS. If it *was* illegal, there would not be the top lawyers and the top law firms in the United States involved.

Pre-Paid Legal has been in this business for **TWENTY-EIGHT YEARS!** They are on the **NEW YORK STOCK EXCHANGE!**

IS THIS NETWORK MARKETING?

You're not one of THOSE, are you? Are you one that HEARD of these *Pyramid Schemes* and how a friend or relative got STUCK in one? Have YOU been in one, and failed? MOST people have. But then, most people fail in LIFE! NETWORK MARKETING has made more MILLIONAIRES in the past two decades than ANY OTHER BUSINESS in the WORLD! In fact, **20% of the MILLIONAIRES in the world** made their millions IN network marketing.

Your BOSS, the guy you work for, is at the top of his *own* pyramid. What are YOUR chances to make more than he makes in that business? If you work really hard, say DOUBLE your hours at work, could you ever be where he (or she) is?

And with network marketing, do you think that radio and TV ads aren't network marketing? Do you think that EVERYONE in ANY business, doesn't MARKET their wares through some kind of *network?* Let me tell you HOW network marketing REALLY works. I've studied it for FORTY YEARS and network marketed my HOW NOT TO BE LONELY book.

I went out and made speeches. I worked with clubs and gave THEM a commission for selling my books; their club made money and I sold books. I went through a distributor who put my books in retail book stores. THEY sold my books. It was ALL one big NETWORK of people MARKETING my book. And I was at the TOP of that legal *pyramid* because I worked the hardest!

MOST people fail in network marketing because they either get involved with the *wrong company*, the *wrong vehicle or product*, or they are *lazy*, they never take the time to *learn* about the product, they won't follow the *proven system*, or they QUIT!

First of all, a pyramid SCHEME is illegal. Around Christmas all sorts of "get rich quick" deals spring up everywhere with someone calling or writing asking you to send money—CASH money—to someone else. If you do, they say you WILL get 10 or 100 times what you sent back in a few weeks.

The truth is, this HAS happened to some but *most* just throw the money away and *somebody* HAS to be stuck in the end. You have no PRODUCT! NO service; just people sending MONEY to others. **This is illegal!** PLEASE, don't confuse network marketing with an illegal pyramid.

People who network market work HARD! They find a product or service, they *learn* about the product and they *tell others* about it. When they find others who want to ALSO *tell* about the product, they train them; they DUPLICATE themselves, they *network,*

and they make a RESIDUAL income. It is how MIL-
LIONAIRES are made from *scratch.* It is your own
home-based business.

What genuinely *good all over* feeling it is to be
able to SPEND "almost" what you want; to be able to
buy a new car and not haggle (a lot) on the price, to be
able to read that menu from left to right, not caring
WHAT the price of the meal is, and to choose the
vacation you WANT, not the one you can *afford.*

BUT, it takes HARD work, it takes SMART work,
and it takes the right PRODUCT to market. You need
training and you need to follow "the system." Far too
many want to try it THEIR way and most of the time,
"their way" is incorrect. If you have a successful
company you represent, if its product and those who
are successful with marketing that product or service
worked the way they were taught, why not TRY to do
it their way?

Let's look at some people who are making big
money in their own home-based business. They are
from all over the United States and from every walk of
life. Some were successful before but are MORE
successful now. Some are college educated, some
are not. What they ALL have in common is the DE-
SIRE TO BETTER THEMSELVES.

They were willing to TRY! They were willing to
LEARN! They were willing to WORK! They BELIEVED
in themselves and they BELIEVED in their product.
MOST started PART-TIME. They KEPT "*beans on the
table*" while they TRIED to improve their financial life.
AND, they ALL made it!

Chapter 2

SUCCESSFUL PEOPLE

Remember earlier when I said, *"If you wanted to get SKINNY it's a waste of time to talk with FAT people. And if you want to get RICH, why listen to the advice of those who are POOR?"* I wasn't trying to be cute or hurtful, it's just facts; it's THE WAY IT IS!

There is no DOUBT, that if more people were AWARE of *Pre-Paid Legal*, if they would sit down and LISTEN to all it can do for them, if they'd READ THIS BOOK and understand WHY *Pre-Paid Legal* is so beneficial, they would join without hesitation.

Consequently, if YOU were to search for a home-based business, what a truly TERRIFIC opportunity this is for YOU to tell others about it; you can HELP people and make a better-than average living to a FORTUNE doing it. It depends on the amount of effort your put forth. It is strange, isn't it, that the people who have the MOST seem to work the hardest (and smartest). How CAN that be?

I know many of you think, *"I can't do this. I'm not a lawyer. I'm not even college educated. Who would believe me?"* Well, you CAN do it. I mean **YOU** can do it if you want to and it is truly a prestigious high potential earning, occupation.

You HELP people from being sued, from having their lives RUINED, and it happens every day to *nice* people, to *good* people, to INNOCENT people and even to smart people.

If they have one of these *Pre-Paid Legal* attorneys or law firms representing them, their chances of losing *diminish,* and their chances of WINNING multiply astronomically. That's not only been proven, it's *common sense!* Do not think—not for a single SECOND—that the color of justice is not GREEN!

The difference in MR. And *"hey you"* is GREEN. Ever get stuck in traffic in a beat-up car and try to squeeze in? NOBODY will let you in. But try it in a Cadillac, Lincoln, Lexus, MERCEDES and watch the people smile as they wave you in to an open spot.

Remember (men and women) those SINGLE days? A member of the opposite sex drives up in a car and they look "nice." If that same person drives up in a RED CONVERTIBLE—with the top down—they are absolutely GORGEOUS!

Let's visit with those who HAVE the expensive cars, the big houses, who go on vacations wherever and whenever they like, and whose kids are in the best colleges. Let's visit with some of the BIG SHOTS in *Pre-Paid Legal* And you, try to identify with them, then close your eyes and think how it COULD be for you if you would only try.

Now, not ALL of these people are "rags to riches" stories and not ALL were failures. But, they apparently were either unhappy with where they *were*, dissatisfied with where they were (or NOT) *going*, they each had the *vision* to see the opportunity, and they WENT FOR IT WITH PASSION. You do NOT get rich HOPING for something. Remember?

Again, the following people are ALL in *Pre-Paid Legal.* MOST, started it part-time. Why couldn't YOU TRY IT **PART-TIME** and see if you are "right" for the job, because it takes a *special kind of person* to be successful in this business.

DAVE SAVULA . . . .

I'm taking Dave FIRST because, in my research into this company, I saw a video with Dave conducting a training session and I LIKED HIM! I liked the way he looked. I liked WHAT he said. And I liked the way he SAID it. Too, he is the TOP MONEY EARNER with *Pre-Paid Legal* and he deserves some special recognition—he EARNED it!

Dave and wife, Bev live on Lake Lanier, in the North Georgia Mountains. In his spare time, Dave coaches football to 7th and 8th kids; he's been doing this for over 25 years. He and Bev were highschool sweethearts; he's known her since she was five. They lived on the same street, 10 houses from each other and they've been married for over 30 years.

They have two sons, David who is 29, a graduate of Georgia State University, and   Mike, 25, a
graduate of The University of Georgia. BOTH work for
major companies and BOTH are Directors in *Pre-Paid
Legal*. Dave and Bev are very proud of their two sons
and of their accomplishments.

Dave travels the country conducting training
sessions, meetings and seminars. When I watched his
tape he motivated ME, and he explains most of what's
in this book in 20 minutes in a clear, fun presentation.
In fact, it is the *best presentation* I have ever heard,
done in simple, non-threatening fashion and he glides
through it with ease and confidence. He has charisma;
you'll like him, too.

Dave "got involved" in *Pre-Paid Legal* in 1985 as
a USER of the plan. It wasn't until seven years later, in
1992, that he got involved "in the business" and he
took off with it at a full run and never stopped.

These "guys" (men and women)I interviewed
talked of earning a six-figure income; NONE told me
what that means. I asked, "Is this six-figure income
have a one in front or a nine?" I feel certain that
Dave's is a *seven*-figure income!

Dave was not a bum looking for a job. He was
part-owner of along distance resale company. But he
wanted to be in business FOR himself and BY himself.
Well, that isn't entirely true. Bev, his wife whom he
brags is the SAME SIZE she was 37 years ago, works
with him.

They LIKE the business because, as Bev puts
it, "*Dave has always done well in business. But with*

Pre-Paid Legal our dream came true. Life is much more stress-free and comfortable without financial worries. Pre-Paid Legal is like life," Bev continues. *"You only get what you give. Give 100 percent and you GET 100 percent. Give ten percent and you GET ten percent."*

It seems that MANY of the successful people in any business work as a team. Dave and Bev operate their business guided by the three R's: They preach AND practice: RESPECT for ones self; RESPECT for others; and RESPONSIBILITY for your business.

I think EVERYONE in *Pre-Paid Legal* has met Dave, or heard him speak in person; certainly they've seen his tape. When I saw it, I felt that my book was a bit inadequate. In fact, the *Pre-Paid Legal* video (Justice For All) is superb. It is, without a doubt, the BEST I have ever seen and I've seen thousands.

Even this great video tape was SECOND to the presentation made by Dave. He talks about . . . NO, I'm not going to tell you; you have to see it for yourself. And you WILL.

SUNIL WADHWA . . . .

I just HAD to interview someone with a name like this. On my call to him, I told him I was writing a book on *Pre-Paid Legal* and his voice grew even MORE interested; I liked HIM right away, too. He had energy, excitement, enthusiasm to burn and we had a conversation about a variety of subjects that lasted more than

40 minutes.

First, I questioned, what kind of name is Sunil (su-neel) Wadhwa (wad-wa)? "Where in the world are you from? You SOUND like a Californian, like your name should be Chad Billingsley or Biff something-or-other." He laughed.

"My dad was in the diplomatic service and is from East India; so is my mother. We traveled all over the world and I ended up married to Lori, an American, and we live in California."

"In 1995 I saw *Pre-Paid Legal* and it was THE chance for us to move ahead with our lives. The very SECOND I saw this, I went for it," he said. "Lori, and I were involved in a business deal in 1990 and we lost $800,000. We spent three YEARS in court fighting for our lives against five individuals who defrauded us.

"I also feel good about myself because even in my small way, I'm making a difference. I am in a position to help others. I can make certain that those who have no legal representation LEARN how to do it through Pe-Paid Legal.

"But I understand you PASSED IT BY the first time you saw it?" I asked.

"This isn't entirely true," he shot back. I LIKED it, I could SEE how I could do it, I just hesitated on the fact that it was Multi-Level Marketing. I had heard so many horror stories about networking "things" that I didn't want to become involved.

"The truth is, like so many who only HEAR MLM or network marketing is a "pyramid scheme" have never been in the industry themselves and only tell you what they HEAR. For those who are AGAINST this type of marketing, they don't HAVE to do it; they can sell the *Pre-Paid Legal* package and make a commission only. They'll just be throwing away most of the money they could earn. Once they learn what it is, they'll change their minds like I did."

JAE HOGLUND . . . .

The Hoglund FAMILY is in *Pre-Paid Legal.* MRS Hoglund works with Jae, and their daughters, Heather and Heidi, are also Director Level Associates. As is the case with most of the successful people who are in any type of business, the *spouse* is a strong part of it all. In this case, Jackie, Jae's wife, is there for him and there *with* him. Opposites attract ONLY in physics.

When a husband AND wife see an opportunity they both believe in, that they can work it as a couple, it is usually successful and if not, they did it *together*!

Jae and Jackie were MEMBERS of PPL for 10 years before (you guessed it) *Dave Savula* motivated them to try as associates. "Reluctantly," Jae said, "I joined. Being members for ten years I had all good experiences with the service, I could see the NEED others would have for it, so we went for it."

Of course, I was making a living as a job recruiter and I kept it. This new thing with *Pre-Paid Legal* was to *see* if it worked to defray the monumental expense of sending both daughters to college. As a job recruiter I knew I could talk with people and this seemed reasonable.

"Well, when the first $500 week came around, it kind of got my attention. Remember, I was just "playing" with the business. When the checks multiplied to $500 a DAY, we went at it full-time and have NEVER LOOKED BACK!

"It's a great feeling to be able to develop your own retirement income without risk of downsizing, of being fired and having to DRIVE to and from work each day. And of course, if I don't feel like going to work I just stay home. Actually, there is no great benefit of doing that because home is WHERE I work!

"I know that others in this business say this and I can empathize with them because I feel the EXACT way about HELPING people. The money part is terrific. It changed our lives so wonderfully well. But helping others achieve *their* financial dreams is so very rewarding, too. I sleep well at night.

"And, I've made some very strong *business* relationships in and working with others on PPL that have developed into very strong *personal* relationships. When a bunch of us and our wives get together at a regional or national convention, it's like a high-school reunion."

CLEVE PICKENS . . . .

Another character, I thought. I was right. Cleve and his wife Dulcie live in Windermere, Florida and they have two children, Cricket and Wes—both in *Pre-Paid*

Legal. "Why not?" Cleve Smiles, "it has made me and Dulcie a good life. We have a lake home we bought to enjoy on weekends. I was close to bankruptcy when *Pre-Paid* came into my life.

Now, I have a six-figure income (they ALL say that! I need to ask is that with a 1, 2, 5, NINE?), my kids are attending the college of their choice. In fact, we have THREE homes, and we are living our dream. If I hadn't become involved with *Pre-Paid*, I don't even want to THINK what I'd be doing.

"Is it hard to sell anybody? Not for me," Cleve answers himself. "All I do is hand out Dave's (Savula's) *Secret's Out* tape with a PPL brochure and my business card all held together by a rubber band and wait for the calls.

"Believe it! It is THAT simple. If people KNOW about *Pre-Paid Legal*, they join. Once they join and see how easy it was for me to get THEM to join as a member, they almost all recognize that it is also a future for them doing as I do. I love this service," Cleve adds. "I am making a *difference.*"

THE DORSEY'S . . . .

NO, not Jimmy and Tommy (for those of you old enough to remember), MIKE and MICHAEL Dorsey —the *top* father-and-son team in *Pre-Paid Legal.*

Mike, the father, has been in PPL since 1985 as a member, but not until 1996 when he and son Michael were actively looking for a business they could work together did they learn that *Pre-Paid Legal* offered a network marketing plan; their search was over.

"Everything fell into perfect order," Mike said. "We were convinced that *PPL* was the right company, certainly they had the right *product*, at the right price *and* the right profit potential."

"ANYONE can do this business," Michael states with a smile. "We had tried other network marketing companies, we KNEW the power of network marketing, but with *Pre-Paid Legal*, it ALL scored perfect marks. We were RIGHT! The ONLY way anyone can fail in this company is if they don't TRY!

What do they earn? I found them in the book of leaders and it states that they are $250,000 "ring earners." It doesn't mean ONLY $250,000, it means a *minimum* of that much. They've shared this honor for three years in a row.

Mike and wife, Lola, make their home in Duluth, Georgia. Michael and his wife, Amy, are in Suwanee, (Georgia, of course). They have two daughters, Alexis and Reese.

MYRNA RILEY . . . .

I taught school for 16 years, but had NO retirement. My husband works in the corporate world and we were transferred frequently; therefore, I was never able to stay in one school system long enough to earn a pension. PLUS, I had always wanted to have my own

business, but I didn't want the headaches of employees, inventories, renting an office or store, putting
in telephones, etc. It's a LOT OF MONEY to start your
own business.

However, I wanted FREEDOM. When I saw *Pre-Paid Legal*, it answered ALL of my problems and was
everything I wanted without the major expense and
headaches. Not only that, I could work from my own
HOME!

And, even though I was in business FOR
myself, I was not in business BY myself. I saw the
chance to sue my teaching skills to teach, my training
skills to help train others, and if I made a sale TODAY
I would get a RENEWAL INCOME the following year.
In other words, if I worked *one* year I could start off my
THIRD year with a monthly income already established. And THIS would provide me with a retirement
account that I had missed with teaching.

I used simple math to figure out what I COULD
make. If I could interest 10 people per month for 10
months (teachers' mentality) for 10 YEARS, that would
add up to be 1,000 sales. If I took the average of $40
per sale and multiply that by 1,000, I could actually
RETIRE ON $40,000 a year!

I decided to TRY; everything seemed good with
nothing to risk but the paltry two-hundred plus dollars.
The rest was up to me. (I PASSED that 1,000 sales
goal I set for myself in TEN months!)

In 1997 my father became seriously ill and was
hospitalized in another state. I could now AFFORD to
take time off to spend with my family through these

difficult times. My dad died. My income while I spent those last weeks with him continued. I even made use of *Pre-Paid Legal* to help solve some problems we were dealing with at his time of death.

I have a profitable business. I am making a difference in people's lives. I have renewal (residual) income. I'm making a nest egg for my children and their families. *Pre-Paid Legal* is a dream come true.

MARK BROWN . . . .

Mark had made a MILLION DOLLARS working with *Pre-Paid Legal* in the past THREE years—starting from *scratch*! I knew he would make a terrific interview. Even before *Regis, MANY People Want To Become A Millionaire!*

In the large PROFILE of SUCCESS book that *Pre-Paid Legal* puts out each year, I was able to pick and choose different people. Mark was a Texan, his wife was gorgeous, I read his success story so I chose him. That "MILLION DOLLARS EARNED IN THREE YEARS" got my attention. Yeah, a good choice.

Since I live on a ranch in Burnet, Texas (pronounced Burn-it) 40 miles west of Austin, I HAD to grab out that map and learn where Weatherford was located (a town near Ft. Worth).

Mark tells how he never earned more than a middle 5-figure income in the printing business and that was about to go under. "You meet MANY people being a printer, and at least once a week *somebody* tried to get me interested in one Multi-Level Marketing company or another. I never went for it because I never *believed* in it and always made a great effort to stay away from any of them.

"But when I saw *Pre-Paid Legal*, I KNEW this one was different. I had never seen a product that made so much sense, or HIT me like this one did. It was, without doubt, a Godsend and, I went for it.

"My dad and I operated this printing business for FIFTEEN YEARS, but when dad died things just weren't the same. I oftentimes dreaded going to work and I was LOOKING for something new. I FOUND IT! With *Pre-Paid Legal* I can't wait to go to work.

"My wife, Denise, works with me side-by-side. My organization is spread over about 50 states and two provinces has well over 200,000 customer-members. This year, it looks like I'm sort of stuck on $40,000 a month. We can live on that pretty well, can't we honey," he winks as he smiles at Denise.

Mark and Denise ARE a team. When he first learned of *Pre-Paid Legal* he and Denise were skeptical. After he attended the convention, he went home and shared it with Denise and she agreed. "Denise was my first and most important sale.

"After that, we were hooked and nothing was going to stop us. It hasn't. It's almost like PRINTING money," he laughs. "And our two children, Candice, 22 is my office manager and Joe, 20, is a computer tech (also an associate).

"Yes, I was *looking* for a new business—*any* business—that required NO inventory, NO employees, no *hassle* in collecting bills. The first six months in *Pre-Paid Legal* I made $40,000; I thought I had died and gone to heaven!

My first FULL year I earned $287,000 (and it hasn't been that bad since). In 1996, one YEAR after I started in the business, I brought in $56,000 in ONE MONTH! Unbelievable, but so wonderfully true."

DAVID BRUERD . . . .

In the *Pre-Paid Legal* brochure there is a photo of David and his young son (looks about two), Austin, and a brown lab named Kodiak. Here is David's story.

David *graduated from college*, but never made much money in whatever he tried. At age 31 he thought he would be a financial *loser* FOREVER. He had never made more than $19,000 a year and the year before he joined *Pre-Paid Legal Services, Inc.* he brought home $13,000.

Even when he got in *Pre-Paid Legal* he didn't work, he admits. His 10th month "just piddlin' with it" he had made a total of $9,631 dollars working it part-time." Somewhere along the way he got serious.

His 14th month he brought in $13,242 for that MONTH alone while he was on vacation in the Caribbean. THEN, *the light bulb was turned on!* The next year David earned over $100,000. He has a new home, a nanny for his son, and best of all David states, "I am never away from my son for more than a few hours. That, in itself, is a huge plus.

He works from his home, and is building a terrific business and a lifelong income. He can go on vacation and REALLY have a great time because when he returns his RESIDUAL income has earned an even LARGER check. What a nice guy and a splendid interview. He deserves success—he's earned it!

LES AND LORIE HARRELL . . . .

"Lorie and I were making good money in the custom jewelry business, but we didn't have a lot of TIME to spend with our family. We had to be *there* to handle customers and again, it was lucrative but we wanted a LIFE. "They have three boys, Ryan, six, Reese, four, and Ridge only a few months old.

"In the nine years we've been married (before PPL) something as simple as decorating the *Christmas tree* was something we couldn't do together —Lorie did it and I worked at the store. Money, as nice as it is to have, isn't everything. Now, we HAVE everything!

"Like many who are associates in *Pre-Paid Legal,* we were *members* first. We had a legal problem that was settled because of our membership and we then looked at the business side. We had never worked in network marketing before. Like Sunil (Wadhwa) we had both *heard* bad things about the industry but these stories are NOT true. They certainly aren't true in *Pre-Paid Legal!*

We now make MUCH MORE than we did in the

jewelry business and we can now decide what *we* want to do with our time. Not having a schedule, we work at out own pace and *when* we want to work. This gives us time to be parents who help out in the class-room, go on field trips with the kids, and spend quality time together.

"Doing something else is unimaginable," Lorie smiles widely. "We can help people with legal prob-lems, be proud as we watch *their* business grow in our company, and we live the life we choose to live." Together they say, "It just doesn't get any better."

DIANNE MOORE/DAVID COMBS ......

PARTNERS! Each married to someone else. David Combs started part-time with *PPL* in November of 1998. He was working as a full-time, teaching golf professional. He had been involved in some form of network marketing for 14 years—not successfully.

However, he KNEW the power and potential of network marketing, he just had never found the right *product* to market. After **trying** *Pre-Paid Legal* for six months, he upped and QUIT his job and went into *PPL* full time. Dianne joined with him in May of 1999.

Dianne started part-time also, and she and David formed a partnership. In just a few days of working together they not only had FUN, they were able to move to the next level by talking with *groups* of employees.

"I had worked as a bookkeeper for the last 17

years," Linda said, "doing the same thing day-after-day. Now I was doing bookkeeping work for my husband's golf club and talking with everyone about the product and the business opportunity. I really WAS having fun helping others and helping myself. I went full-time in January of this year, 2000.

David and I spend most of our time talking with COMPANIES to offer the *Pre-Paid Legal* GROUP plan to their employees (at $14.95 per person). It is both *rewarding and easy* to simply TELL people about something that everyone needs and at a price that is a mere FRACTION of the cost attorneys charge!

Many times we hear things like,"*Where were you three months ago?*" or "*We spent a fortune on this one problem that was more than 20 TIMES the cost of your yearly membership!*" Everyone agrees that "*the color of justice is green*, just as the title of this book states. Well, now, the GREEN is on OUR side and it is a totally comforting and safe feeling."

David and Dianne have to *balance* the time they spend working, and the time they spend with their family. "It's easy to do," they both concur. "We are in BUSINESS FOR OURSELVES! And this *networking* is just terrific! While we're simply *talking* to others we are networking. Many ASK us how *they* can do it and we tell them.

"When we find someone who REALLY wants to try, we train them (we DUPLICATE *ourselves*), THEY make money and WE get an *override* on *their* sales. AND, we are paid year, after year, after year on EVERY sale. The rewards are *sooo* good; we have freedom, travel when we want, where we want, and as often as we like—within reason, of course."

This *team* of David Combs and Dianne Moore have been among the TOP group producers this entire year in our state. "David is number ONE on the list for opening the most groups," Dianne smiles. "It really IS easy representing a company that has been highly successful and has been in business TWENTY-EIGHT YEARS!

"ALL the glitches are worked out in *Pre-Paid Legal,* we are praised and written up by the top magazines in the world, by two stock exchanges, and we HELP people both SAVE money with legal problems and we help them MAKE money simply by telling others about it."

LARRY SMITH . . . .

"In 1996 I was burned out, 45-years old and not a lot of money to invest. I never went to college; had a high school GED and knew that my chances for a good job were not good.

"I started PPL part-time about five hours a week. The turning point in my career was when I brought a $2,000 ring in to a jeweler and the jeweler destroyed it! He knew that by the time I hired a $200 an hour attorney and pursued it legally, that it wasn't worth the investment and I'd let it go. What he didn't know was that I had *Pre-Paid Legal.*

I called my attorney and told her the situation.

With but a single call to the jeweler things happened. The jeweler who, earlier that day told me he couldn't help me, HANDED me a check for $2,152.32. I was HOOKED on *Pre-Paid Legal.*

I reasoned, then and there, that if $25 a month could do that for ME, what could it do for OTHERS? And it just HAD to be easy to interest others if I just TOLD them about it. It has been. I earned $224,000 my SECOND year in the business.

There is PAIN in trying to achieve success; nobody makes big money easily. And, there is PAIN in failure; the only difference is that with success, the pain might be only a year or two whereas the pain of FAILURE lasts a **lifetime!**

As Pete states a time or two (or three) in his book, "It is NOT EASY to get rich, it takes hard, smart work. If it was easy, EVERYBODY would be rich!

Do I LIKE *Pre-Paid Legal?* **I LOVE it!** My "commute" each day is a 15-second jaunt down the stairs to my office, and the only "traffic" is my dog trying to beat me down the stairs. I dress in sweats and a baseball hat most of the time. What a way to work!

JOHN BIRD . . . .

It took me two MONTHS to watch the *Pre-Paid Legal* video and I (now) know I should have watched the tape sooner. Before *Pre-Paid Legal* I managed a 54-hole golf course. I put in from 70 to 90 hours a week and holidays and weekends belonged to the club because THAT'S when the most traffic is there; they are having fun and I am working.

My wife and I BOTH worked, and together we had a good lifestyle, over $100,000 a year but we had no TIME to enjoy our earnings. To keep them we had to KEEP working. But now, with *Pre-Paid Legal*, I make more than that on my own and Jan doesn't have to work anymore.

"*Pre-Paid Legal* gives me the TIME to enjoy my daughter, *Krystina*, who just turned 10. I can attend her school functions, extracurricular activities, and go to father-daughter dances with her; EVERYTHING!

What I like BEST about *Pre-Paid Legal?* Several things: Working at home. Having TIME to do as I please. More income, and a CHANCE to make even MORE. Who wouldn't like that?

RYAN NELSON . . . .

Ryan met Margaret in May of 1997 and they were married in September of 1998. Ryan had traveled the world as a *combustion engineer* but recognized a lifetime opportunity enjoying RESIDUAL income with *Pre-Paid Legal.*

Like everyone else with a JOB, if Ryan worked, he made money. When he wasn't working, his money stopped. This isn't to say that you can work *Pre-Paid Legal* and STOP, but you CAN take a breather now and then and when you come back from say, a two-week vacation in Paris, you have a CHECK waiting and most of the time, it is MORE than the check the few weeks before. THAT is RESIDUAL income! THAT is when you have others working for you that you don't have to PAY!

JOE LEMIRE . . . .

Joe and Ruthie Lemire are *dream seekers*. "For thirty years my wife and I have worked and searched for the lifestyle we now have because of PPL. I was doing very well in the health insurance business, "Joe said, "and in 1993 we bought a *Pre-Paid Legal* membership that we used several times and received quality service.

"I started with it on a part-time basis, but within a year my new PART-time business was making as much as my FULL-time business. That's when Ruthie and I reset out goals and went FULL-TIME.

"Now, we make more money that we can SPEND, and THAT is a terrific feeling. What we like best is we can get in our motor home and travel and write business all over the country. We are HELPING people and making a great living and enjoying it all.

"Our *entire family* is involved in *Pre-Paid Legal*, either as members or associates. Two of our sons, Mike and Phil, are coordinators and as soon as our four grandchildren are old enough they'll be involved.

SPORTS FANS

When I made a few attempts to get Dave Savula on the telephone for an interview, one call I made to his home and his wife, Bev, told me that Dave was visiting with Mr. Tarkenton at his office in downtown Atlanta.

Mr. Tarkenton? There is only *one* person I recall having that name; FRAN Tarkenton, former quarterback of the Minnesota Vikings and New York Giants. I can just *see* him now in my memory's eye, moving right and left, kind of dancing around in that backfield dodging giant-sized defensive lineman.

What I remember mostly about Fran Tarkenton is NOT that he is a HALL OF FAMER, NOT that he passed for over 47 THOUSAND yards as a professional football player **(that's almost 27 MILES!),** but, his *eyes.* His eyes were always wide open looking for a receiver who had but a bit of *daylight* from the defensive back so he could complete a pass. And, his eyes showed NO FEAR!

These *behemoths* who were rushing at him from both sides and crashing down the middle had *one thought* in mind; to tear that quarterback's head *clean off.* I WATCHED this in awe. HIS mission was to win and . . . his eyes showed NO FEAR!

I like to repeat quotes that have meaning; I do it throughout each book I write. One that has a dual meaning is; "*The bigger they are, the harder they fall.*" Cute. Undoubtedly written by someone who has never been in a brawl or a football game with a BIG person. I understand what is being said, but I found that, "*The bigger they are, the harder they HIT.*" I think Fran Tarkenton will agree with me on that point.

When Fran Tarkenton was playing matador to those charging bulls, he was six feet tall and weighed about 185 pounds. Not big when being actively pursued by a ferocious GANG of 280 pounders (or more). He was the ultimate scrambler. His prime concern was to get that ball to a receiver and win the game.

Most of the time, within fractions of a second from when he released the ball, he was hit—hard—by one, two or *three* of those fast, oversized giants. Many times they fell ON him or he was *rolled on* AFTER the hit. Of course he KNEW this, but completing that pass was his ultimate goal.

His reactions were either he smiled and jumped up because it was a completion, or he shook his head and kicked turf because it wasn't. The fact is, you can't beat a guy like that. The pain never figured into his equation. Yeah, I watched his *eyes*.

AND, to my delight, I learned that Fran Tarkenton is a stockholder in *Pre-Paid Legal* and also WORKS THE BUSINESS! For you football fans who "team up" with *Pre-Paid Legal,* YOU will be on the same team as *Fran Tarkenton*!

Now this won't make you any more money, and if you bring a football for him to autograph for your kid (or yourself) it won't make you any more successful. But bet on the fact that if I am at a meeting or function where he's present, I'll (unashamedly) ask to have a picture taken with him.

Chapter 3

QUESTIONS AND ANSWERS

Q If I want to become involved working in *Pre-Paid Legal*, what is my next step?

A Talk to the person who gave you this book. Their name SHOULD be in the back.

Q How much does it cost to join?

A You mean to start your own home-based business? $249 total.

Q What do I GET for this money and what MORE is there to spend?

A A complete information and starting PACKET that enables to make money IMMEDIATELY!

Q Will I have to attend meetings?

A If you're smart you will. Not only will you learn more about *Pre-Paid Legal* but you'll also learn how to conduct your OWN meetings if you choose.

Q You mean I don't have to GO to meetings unless I choose?

A NOPE! But, you should WANT to. These meetings aren't long, they aren't dull, you meet others who are starting, ones at different stages of their business, and you'll LEARN.

Q Do I have to drag my friends (prospects) to meetings?

A In MOST instances THAT is difficult to do. . . UNLESS you tell them about *Pre-Paid Legal.* Most WANT to learn more once you've whet their appetite. But DO *drag* them to a meeting if Dave Savula gives it; his presentations are truly awesome.

Q You make it sound easy. It can't be *that* easy. If it was, everybody would be doing it.

A Everybody (probably) WOULD be doing it if they KNEW about it. RARELY is earning big money easy. It takes time, and effort, and organizational skills. When you're tired, instead of resting, WORK. Do it often enough and long enough and you'll be rich.

Q How long will it take for me to make $100,000?

A As soon as you sell 750 memberships. MANY (who work at it diligently) make that in eight to 10 months or less.

Q Is it difficult to sell people on this *Pre-Paid Legal* plan as a *member?*

A You mean to interest someone in a *membership?* That answer is **NO!** It's a *piece of cake* as long as you explain it to them or they consent to watch the company video (or Dave's tape).

Q How about becoming an ASSOCIATE?

A Not every MEMBER joins as an associate. When they DO, they (usually) begin part-time unless they are able to see "the big picture" right away.

Q Can YOU earn a living representing *Pre-Paid Legal* as an associate?

A Only YOU can answer that. Hard, smart work and the right VEHICLE spells success.

Q Can you interest others in doing it, too?

A **YES!** EVERYBODY wants extra income and this is not SELLING, it's simply TELLING! (TIP: USE THIS BOOK; IT sells *for* you!)

Q This is like selling INSURANCE, isn't it?

A Well, *kinda'.* The BIG difference is that friends and relatives don't run AWAY from you. They hear what you're doing and they WANT to know more.

Q How difficult is it to sell?

A First, you only TELL; there is no need to SELL. To do this, you must LEARN. You must STUDY. You must LISTEN to tapes, read and watch a few good videos then, DO IT!

That's why it's smart to go to meetings. When the meeting is over, people gather in little "bunches" and ask and answer questions. It's fun to listen and learn this way. Of course, I like people and this always helps. And you ARE *helping* people, too. That's part of my next chapter—the last one, I think. It's called . . .

MAKE A *GRAND* LIVING
MAKE A *GIANT* DIFFERENCE

What a truly superb home-based business this is for most; inexpensive to join, easy to learn, fun to talk about, and just about EVERYONE is a prospect. All of a sudden, people are LISTENING to you; they WANT to know more about it.

We all agree that MOST people fail in LIFE! MOST people, even the ones who work *Pre-Paid Legal* PART-TIME, do NOT fail. IF of course, they don't quit and if they have a *planned program, a system*. Follow it, put in the time, and the LONGER you do this the more money you make.

REMEMBER, you get renewal's year after year of what you do NOW, as long as the person keeps their coverage; most DO! BECAUSE it is NEEDED, it is inexpensive, and it can make your life a lot more enjoyable, more secure.

Here's that word again—*litigious*—this is one LITIGIOUS society with everybody suing everybody else for the strangest of reasons. Remember, too, you have a THREE TIMES greater chance of needing an attorney than you do of going to the hospital.

If you WANT AN OPPORTUNITY to get rich, work *Pre-Paid Legal* hard and smart. Put in the time. **Follow the system!** Accept help from those who are successful; there are many of them and many WILL help if you ask for it. It relieves the stress of "want" because you will NEVER want again.

First, you call the person who told you about being a MEMBER of *Pre-Paid Legal* and ask THEM. If they're done their "job" right, chances are they've already told you. If not, call them back and ask about working this as a home-based business.

Again, you and I both know that very few (if ANY) people who have a J-O-B will get rich. Oh, if you have the same job for years, chances are you're making some decent money but NEVER will you make enough working for someone else where you'll become RICH! It rarely happens that way.

Perhaps you can make some investments but on WAGES, most of your income is taken up with everyday living expenses. You simply MUST be in business for yourself to make it big.

Hey, if you're satisfied with your regular job, if you're happy, if your family is provided for and you can see your way clear to live off your retirement, stay where you are! Be happy and may God bless you!

BUT, if you're kind of STUCK in that "financial quagmire," you are in a rut. A RUT is the same as a GRAVE but with a rut, there are two ways out. I'm offering you a way out now. I'm not insulting you or hurting your feelings and I'm explaining so you will understand that THIS is a grand opportunity for many.

In a recent book I re-wrote titled THE NEW MILLIONAIRES, I talk about home-based businesses. In fact the subtitle is PYRAMID SCHEMES vs. HOME-BASED BUSINESSES because I'm in FAVOR OF network marketing companies and people working at home, people TRYING to get ahead, people making an attempt to change their financial lives.

If you are EXPOSED to a good product (*PPL*), with a good company (*PPL*), with a good pay plan (*PPL*), that benefits the masses (*PPL*), you have the company to work for (*Pre-Paid Legal*). If you Network, you clone yourself, you DUPLICATE yourself. *Pre-Paid Legal* has ALL of this.

Is it a pyramid? I think so. My MOTHER is a pyramid; she's at the top of our family and we are all below her. A college DEAN is a pyramid; the professors work for him, the janitors keep things clean for the professors, the students LEARN and on and on. A CEO is at the TOP of his "pyramid."

What these *naive* folks call a pyramid is when somebody asks them to send a hundred bucks to five other people and they expect to get a hundred bucks back from a *hundred* other people; SOMEBODY gets bumped in the end.

Want to INSULT the boobs who call it a pyramid? Get a copy of THE NEW MILLIONAIRES, I
barbecue these imbeciles throughout the book because they, in their total ignorance, will HURT others
from being successful. They (mostly) *mean* well (I
think), they just DON'T KNOW THAT THEY DON'T
KNOW. They voice their unfounded, unwise, un
KNOWING opinion and prevent MANY from being
financially successful in the LEGITIMATE business of
Network Marketing.

Yes, EVERY business is a "pyramid," where the
boss is at the top of the "pyramid" and makes the most
money. HERE is a chance for YOU to be your own
boss in your own home-based business.

MAKE BIG MONEY FAST

HERE is something exciting I almost left out; **GROUP
SALES**. Millie Baker of Tulsa, Oklahoma, is part of the
Pre-Paid Legal GROUP MARKETING TEAM! **Her
income last year was in excess of $225,000!**

"It didn't take me long to figure out that since I
was I already working in schools (her husband and
partner, BAKE, is a high school principal), I could get
with the principal, teachers, maintenance, cafeteria
and maintenance workers into *PPL.* For $14.95 a
month each I could get the BEST legal counsel in
Oklahoma for these folks.

"EVERYBODY gets sued or needs legal advice
(certainly a WILL) and papers to look over no matter

what they do. This helps THEM, and I make a terrific living HELPING others."

"If you talk to a group of say 100 people in a school, factory, large office—anyplace—and just HALF of them join (they almost ALL do) You've earned $3,000 in one morning or one afternoon. When they renew, you make that same amount AGAIN, and again, and again!

"In other words, you start off NEXT year with the same commissions as you made this year. It doesn't take a rocket scientist to figure out how much you *might* make in five or ten years. THINK about it; you can OFFER this plan to a group of five or more for $14.95 per month per person." Now, let's see if YOU can do it by answering a few questions in this test.

1. Do you have a job?
If you answer **YES** or **NO**, it makes no difference.

2. Do you LIKE your job?
If you answered YES **or** NO here makes no difference either. Even if you HATE it and NEED it to support your family, you have NO choice but to keep it. And, even if you LOVE your job, how *about* the pay?

3. Are you making sufficient MONEY on this job?
THIS answer is almost always **NO!** FEW feel they are making the money they deserve or would like to have.

4. Would you like to earn MORE MONEY?
This is a *no-brainer.* Almost EVERYONE would like

MORE money.

5. Are you willing put in 30-35 hours a week, PART-TIME, TRYING something new?

This is probably THE most important answer so far because many of you failed in MLM or NM before. You WANTED a change and you listened to that silk suit in front of the room who said you could make thousands a week by doing little or nothing. It takes HARD, SMART work (with a little luck and proper timing thrown in) to become wealthy.

6. Are you willing to take the time to study and learn?

There is a definite need for a **YES** here because to sell anything—even to TELL people anything—you have to KNOW WHAT YOU'RE TALKING ABOUT!

7. How ABOUT giving *Pre-Paid Legal* a try? Think you could do it? Would you like an OPPORTUNITY to make as much as you feel you deserve?

Of course, three **YES** answers means you ARE ready to TRY.

My *mission* is to help people reach their potential, to help those who will take the time, make the effort, and who WANT to change their financial life FOREVER. I hope you can "see the big picture." I want you NEVER to have to read that menu from right to left ever again! You'll remember this and smile when *you're there*.

You don't NEED a college degree, you don't HAVE to be trained in ANYTHING, you don't NEED a lot of money to TRY; what you need is GUTS, the DESIRE to become financially independent, and the WILL to make it happen. *Pre-Paid Legal* is a smooth road to financial independence.

Money has but ONE sense and that is HEAR-ING. If you tell it *right,* it makes money for you. And if you tell it *wrong*, you LOSE money. If you CALL IT loudly enough, if you WANT it and not WISH for it, you'll get it. I feel that *Pre-Paid Legal* is a bright and shiny VEHICLE and a terrific OPPORTUNITY for many to change their life and lifestyle FOREVER. It isn't for everyone but it MIGHT be for you. *"Don't TAKE a chance, you'll never HAVE a chance*."

Whatever your choice, I wish you well. I PUSH-ED a mite in this book because I truly want to *guide* those who WANT more out of life to get it. I FOUND *Pre-Paid Legal*. It took me 28 years but, I FOUND IT! And now, I want YOU, if you're looking for a home-based business, to give *Pre-Paid Legal* a chance to help you change *your* financial life for the better.

PLEASE, look at the following page. IF so many NEED *Pre-Paid Legal*, If (every year) there are so many more lawsuits, and if so many do not KNOW about *Pre-Paid Legal*, it looks like an "*easy sell*" to me. Remember, *"If it is to BE, it is up to ME."*

Good luck and God bless.

Pete Billac

THE NEED
FOR PRE-PAID LEGAL SERVICES

In 1980 there were
12 MILLION
court filings across America.

In 1998 there were nearly
100 MILLION
court filings across America.

In 2000—TODAY—EVERYBODY
needs a lawyer.

LAWYERS cost a LOT of MONEY.

YOU can have the BEST for $25 a MONTH.

It is SMART to become a MEMBER!

It is WISE to try as a PROFESSION!

DO YOU THINK THERE MIGHT BE A
NEED
FOR PRE-PAID LEGAL SERVICES
IN YOUR LIFE?

ABOUT THE AUTHOR

PETE BILLAC is one of the most sought-after speakers in the United States. This is his 50th book; 45 have become BESTSELLERS. His worldwide best seller, HOW NOT TO BE LONELY, sold over FIVE million copies in three years. His books are published in 31 languages.

Pete is a maverick; he writes what pleases him. His topics range from adventure to war, the Mafia, famous people, to romance, love, health, motivation and self-help.

He speaks to Fortune 500 companies on marketing, he lectures at universities across America, and delivers his "message" at conventions and seminars around the world. For fun, he conducts lectures on cruise ships.

Pete is currently traveling the world with his newest book, *JUSTICE IS GREEN (Pre-Paid Legal)*. "*This book does two things; gets people a top-notch attorney they can easily afford , and tells them how to get out of their financial quagmire. Making money is great—and easy, too, if you believe in yourself and work smart. God wants you to be prosperous, and to help others along the way.*"

Perhaps you've seen Pete on Donahue, Sally Jessy Raphael, Good Morning America, Laff Stop or other national televison shows. He mixes common sense and knowledge with laughter. He charms his audiences with his quick wit and candor, and breathes life into every topic. He makes his audiences laugh—hard!

"Pete is an expert at restoring self-confidence and self-esteem in others . . ."

Phil Donahue
National Television Talk Show Host

Justice is Green

Pre-Paid Legal

is available in quantity discounts through:

LONGEVITY MEDIA
PMB 236
18402 North 19ᵗʰ Ave.
Phoenix, AZ 85023

www.longevitymedia.com
email: info@longevitymedia.com

Phone: 623-434-5119
Fax: 888-515-5299

For information on Pre-Paid Legal:

After reading this book, please pass it on to a friend or relative. It could change their lives for the better—FOREVER.